THE MOVIE STORYBOOK

WALT DISNEY PICTURES presents

WARREN BEATTY

DICK TRACY

Original Score by DANNY ELFMAN

Editor RICHARD MARKS

Production Designer RICHARD SYLBERT

Cinematography by VITTORIO STORARO, A.I.C.-A.S.C.

Co-Producer JON LANDAU

Executive Producer BARRIE M. OSBORNE

Screenplay by JIM CASH & JACK EPPS, JR. and BO GOLDMAN & WARREN BEATTY

Produced and Directed by WARREN BEATTY

Soundtrack Album Available On Warner Bros. Records

Produced in association with
SILVER SCREEN PARTNERS IV

Dolby Stereo® Selected Theatres

Distributed by Buena Vista Pictures Distribution, Inc.

© 1990 THE WALT DISNEY COMPANY

Storybook adapted by JUSTINE KORMAN

Illustrated with photographs from the film

A GOLDEN BOOK • NEW YORK
Western Publishing Company, Inc., Racine, Wisconsin 53404

"Calling Dick Tracy...Calling Dick Tracy!" Detective Dick Tracy's wrist-radio crackled in the opera house.

"Not again," said Tracy's girlfriend, Tess Trueheart.

"I'll be back to see how it comes out," Tracy whispered. Then he raced to the scene of the crime.

"We don't have the slightest clue who any of these men are," complained Police Chief Brandon, baffled by the sudden slaying of five men in the Seventh Street Garage. Officers Pat Patton and Sam Catchem agreed.

To their amazement, crack detective Dick Tracy instantly recognized the faces of the slain gangsters: Little Face, the Rodent, Shoulders, the Brow, and Stooge Villers.

On the wall, written in bullet holes, Tracy read his own name. The courageous detective took the warning as a challenge.

"They all knew Lips Manlis," Tracy concluded. "And I'll bet my badge that Big Boy Caprice is behind this."

True to his promise, Tracy returned in time to see the end of the opera. When he left that evening, he was mobbed by reporters.

"Any comment on the rumour you're moving up to chief of police?" shouted one reporter.

"We already have an excellent police chief," Tracy answered.

Later, on the way to Mike's Diner, Tess was concerned. "Chief Brandon says you'd make a wonderful chief of police. Why don't you want the job?"

"I know the job is safer, and I could sure use the extra forty bucks a week, but nobody is going to put Big Boy behind bars sitting behind a desk," Tracy said. Tess wanted Tracy to take a less dangerous job, but someday she'd have to accept that catching criminals would always be more important to him than promotions, salary, and even his own safety.

"If only I could catch Big Boy!" thought Tracy. The criminal mastermind had the City in his fist, and his grip was tightening.

Tracy pulled open the door to Mike's Diner and collided with a ragged-looking boy who was being pursued by an old man.

"He took my watch!" the old man cried.

Tracy took off after the boy. The breathless chase led to a railroad yard where the boy disappeared behind a passing train. Tracy followed the sound of voices to a dingy shack.

"What'd ya get?" a rough voice demanded.

"Ya didn't save me no chicken?" the boy complained.

"Let's see the stuff!" the rough voice said.

The boy gave the old man's watch to the tramp. Not satisfied, the tramp knocked the boy to the floor.

"Hey, tough guy, why don't you try that on me?" Dick Tracy challenged from the shack's doorway.

The tramp looked up, astonished. He soon found himself on the business end of Tracy's fist, and then Tracy clamped handcuffs on him.

"What're you gonna do to me?" the boy asked worriedly.

"I don't know. Let's have the watch," Tracy replied. "Is this guy your old man?"

"Him? Go soak your head," the boy sneered.

"Let's go. I've got a cell waiting for you," Tracy told the tramp, who glared at him.

"Who are you, mister?" the tramp snarled.

"I'm a cop."

Meanwhile, at the elegant
Club Ritz, Lips Manlis, the
owner, savoured the performances
of stunning singer Breathless
Mahoney and her piano player,
88 Keys.

Wearing a tuxedo, a rose in
his lapel, Lips was sipping
expensive champagne.

As Breathless finished her
song a beefy bodyguard
whispered to Lips, "Bad news at
the garage, boss. They bumped
off everybody. Our boys are
gettin' awful nervous."

Lips frowned, but he quickly
hid his displeasure when
Breathless came over to his table.

Just then a customer screamed,
"Raid! It's the cops!"

All of a sudden uniformed policemen charged in and arrested Lips
Manlis for operating an illegal gambling house. But Lips wasn't
worried until the "police officers" ushered him outside and he saw
gangland assassin Flattop in their unmarked car.

"Hello, Lips," said Flattop, who was holding a tommy gun.

"Hey, you guys ain't cops," Lips sputtered.

The car sped away, followed by an alert veteran cop who had
noticed the uniformed police officers in the unmarked car.

Later, Lips lay sprawled on the grimy floor of the Southside Warehouse, his attempted escape stopped by Big Boy's ruthless thugs.

"Aw, look what you done to your pretty tuxedo," said Big Boy Caprice, cracking walnuts in his powerful fist.

"Big Boy, ain't we pals?" Lips whimpered.

"No pals in this business," Big Boy said. "You taught me that. Sign it!" He handed Lips a pen and a legal document turning the Club Ritz over to Big Boy. In exchange, with gangster gratitude, Big Boy gave Lips a pair of cement overshoes.

Outside, the veteran cop reported strange goings-on at the Southside Warehouse. At the police headquarters switchboard, alert Sam Catchem called Dick Tracy…

who at that moment was enjoying a piece of pie at Mike's Diner with Tess and the young watch thief. The hungry boy was stuffing his face greedily, slurping and gulping to Tess's dismay.

"You got a name?" Detective Tracy wondered.

"Kid," the boy replied between bites.

"What's the name your mother and father gave you?" Tracy said.

The Kid chewed furiously. "What mother and father?"

"Who takes care of you?" Tess asked, concerned.

"Who takes care of *you*?" he snapped with a tough-guy shrug.

When Tracy decided to call the orphanage, the Kid ran for the door. Tracy grabbed him and sat him back down at the table.

"You ain't sticking me in no orphanage," the Kid declared.

"Sorry, pal, it's the law," Tracy said. "What's so bad about the orphanage? They feed you and give you clothes, and…"

"Maybe they'll give you a bath," Tess added hopefully.

"Forget the bath, Kid. What you want is some lamb chops and potatoes, and how about some ice cream?" Tracy suggested just as his wrist-radio crackled with Sam Catchem's call.

Tracy raced to the Southside Warehouse. The veteran cop couldn't identify the men he saw, but Tracy spotted a sapphire earring sparkling on the grime-streaked floor, along with several walnut shells—two more pieces in the puzzle that could add up to Big Boy behind bars. Tracy knew Big Boy loved walnuts. He ordered Sam to bring in Big Boy's men—Flattop, Itchy, and Mumbles. He instructed Pat to get some fingerprints from the walnut shells.

"What have Big Boy's triggermen got to do with walnut shells?" Pat wondered.

Tracy didn't take time to explain. "We've got to find Lips Manlis. Fast."

For many long hours, Tracy grilled Big Boy's men. A thirsty Mumbles squirmed under the hot lights and the painted gaze of an innocent-looking ceramic polar bear as Tracy repeatedly asked him where Lips Manlis was.

"Where is Lips Manlis?" Tracy asked him for the last time, pouring a glass of water from the polar-bear cooler.

Mumbles finally cracked. "Biboyklldlpsmnlis," he confessed.

"That's his testimony," Tracy said to the bewildered stenographer. "We're bringing in Big Boy!"

Dick Tracy took Flattop and Itchy to the Club Ritz.

"Here's your garbage," Tracy told Big Boy. "Where's Lips?"

Big Boy cracked a walnut. "He left town or something. I own the club now. We made a deal."

"You like walnuts, don't you?" Tracy asked him.

"Walnuts are good for the liver," Big Boy said.

"But bad for the brain," Tracy added. "I'm arresting you for the murders at the Seventh Street Garage and of Lips Manlis."

Pat and Sam dragged Big Boy away. Then Breathless spoke up. "Aren't you going to arrest me?"

Tracy noticed a single sapphire earring twinkling on her ear. "I want you to tell me in court who killed Lips Manlis," Tracy declared. But Breathless refused.

The next day Big Boy strutted out of City Hall after being cleared of murder due to lack of evidence. "Police brutality, boys," Big Boy proclaimed to the swarm of reporters.

A reporter approached District Attorney Fletcher and asked, "Will you take disciplinary action against Detective Tracy?"

"I think Detective Tracy has been under a lot of strain," Fletcher answered carefully.

Later, in Fletcher's office, both Tracy and Chief Brandon were scolded by the D.A.

"I'm a candidate for mayor," Fletcher said. "You can't arrest people for murder without proper evidence. Chief, if you can't control Detective Tracy, you'll just have to take him off duty."

That afternoon Tracy and Tess took the Kid shopping for new clothes. Unhappy with the stiff suit Tess chose for him, the Kid bolted out of the store in his underwear. Tracy followed close at his heels and caught him at the corner.

"Are you going to run away every time somebody says something you don't like?" Tracy asked. "You need new clothes. If you don't like the ones Tess picked out, pick out what you want."

Tracy and the Kid went back inside, unaware of Flattop and Itchy lurking in a parked car across the street.

After a ride in the country, Tracy, Tess, and the Kid parked outside Tess's apartment building. On the steps, the detective tried to get up the nerve to ask Tess to marry him.

Before he could pop the question, the Kid cried, "Look out!"

A car without its lights on squealed by, and bullets sprayed from a tommy gun. "Merry Christmas, copper!" someone yelled.

Tracy pulled Tess to safety, and the Kid huddled on the floor of Tracy's car as the gangsters roared off.

"Thanks for the tip, Kid," Tracy told the boy.

"I thought we were goners," the Kid said breathlessly.

"They're just trying to scare us," Tracy declared.

"I'm sorry, Tess," he added. But the still-shaken Tess Trueheart wasn't sure she could live with Dick Tracy's dangerous job.

Later, at Tracy's office, the Kid slept while the detective studied photos of cars resembling the one driven by the gangsters. Tracy looked up as Breathless Mahoney sauntered into the room.

"I'm so glad you called," she said warmly. "I was beginning to wonder what a girl has to do to get arrested."

When Tracy didn't respond to her flirting, Breathless turned to leave. "You're right, Tracy. Why would you get mixed up with someone like me? I'll be lucky if I get through the week alive. They probably followed me here."

Pat and Sam saw Breathless in the hallway as she was leaving. Tracy grabbed his coat and dashed out, yelling back to the officers, "Boys, watch the Kid."

With the Kid safely at the station, Tracy followed Breathless, just as she had planned.

Breathless led Tracy to the Club Ritz. When Tracy saw two of Big Boy's men, he called Sam and Pat and told them to get there fast. He climbed onto a second-story ledge as his buddies arrived in their car.

In the club's top-floor conference room Big Boy was presiding over a gathering of gangland leaders that included Pruneface, Johnny Ramm, Spud Spaldoni, and other kings of crime.

Tracy spoke into his wrist-radio. "I can't hear a thing, Pat. We're going to need a microphone. But if I'm right about what's happening, we'll have to move quickly. I'm coming down."

Inside, Big Boy announced his plan for all the gangsters to form one big criminal company, with himself in charge.

"Why you?" Spud Spaldoni objected. But Big Boy wasn't in the mood for a discussion. Spud left the club in anger and climbed into his waiting limousine.

Before the horrified eyes of Tracy, Pat, and Sam, Spaldoni's limo exploded in a burst of flames. All of the gangsters except Big Boy rushed to a window of the conference room.

"Very upsetting," said Big Boy while the others looked at the wreckage nervously. After seeing what happened to Spaldoni, the rest of the gangsters agreed to go along with Big Boy's plan.

Before he could be discovered, Tracy leapt from the ledge to a lamppost and slid down, landing on the roof of a parked car. Then he jumped onto the top of Pat and Sam's car as it sped past the burning limousine.

No one saw a faceless observer wearing a large hat and a coat step out of the shadows to watch Tracy escape. The mysterious person was the Blank.

The next morning rain poured down outside the window of Tracy's apartment. The detective astonished his guest, the Kid, by brushing his teeth.

"Tracy, for a tough guy, you do a lot of pansy things," the Kid said as he fiddled with a baseball.

"It's peppermint. Try some," Tracy urged.

Just then there was a knock at the door.

Tracy asked who it was, and a voice answered, "It's Mrs. Skaff from the Welfare Department. It has come to our attention that you have an orphan with you. He belongs in an orphanage."

Stalling for time, Tracy put the chain on the door.

Thunder boomed and lightning crackled as the Kid made a desperate decision to escape a grim fate.

While Tracy and Mrs. Skaff argued through the closed door, the Kid scrambled into his clothes. Then he took Tracy's wallet, his badge, and the baseball, and he slipped through the bedroom window and out onto the fire escape.

"Don't force me to get a court order," Mrs. Skaff said just as the detective noticed the Kid was gone.

Tracy opened the door. "Just leave the Kid to me. I'll take care of—"

Instead of Mrs. Skaff, Tracy was surprised to find Itchy, who had been imitating a woman's voice.

"We don't want no kid, copper," Flattop said as he and Itchy grabbed Tracy.

In the alley below, the Kid was thinking about his decision to leave when he saw Flattop and Itchy force Tracy into a car. The Kid jumped onto the back bumper of the car and held on tight as the car roared away.

Flattop and Itchy took Tracy to the basement of Tess's apartment building, where Big Boy and Numbers were waiting.

The Kid jumped off the car and sneaked over to the basement window to see what was happening.

"We thought you might be more comfortable meeting us here, Tracy," Big Boy said, cracking some walnuts in his hands as he looked around. "Too bad it's such a dump. If you were on my payroll, your girlfriend could live in a much nicer place."

Big Boy took out a large roll of money from his pocket. "All yours, Tracy," he said. "I want you on my side."

"This is a lot of dough, Big Boy," Tracy said.

The Kid gasped. Would Tracy take a bribe?

Tracy threw the money in Big Boy's face, exclaiming, "You are guilty of attempting to bribe an officer of the law!"

"You dumb cop!" snarled Big Boy. "You're gonna have a terrible accident!"

Flattop and Itchy tied Tracy to a chair and placed it near the furnace.

"When Itchy knocks the safety valve off this furnace, you're gonna be chop suey. You wanna change your mind?" Big Boy asked the detective.

"Why? What's the matter with Chinese food?" Tracy replied.

"So long, sucker. You shoulda made the deal," Big Boy sneered, climbing the stairs with Numbers as Itchy started pounding the valve on the furnace with a large wrench.

After Itchy and Flattop left, Tracy saw the Kid peering through the grimy window. "Kid!" he yelled. "Get out of here! This place is going to blow!"

Although the Kid was frightened, he hurled his baseball through the window with a mighty crash. The blow sent jagged pieces of glass flying into the basement. Then he climbed through the window and jumped to the floor.

While the whole floor shuddered under their feet, the Kid helped Tracy cut the ropes with a piece of glass. Then, just seconds before the furnace exploded, Tracy and the Kid made it up the basement stairs and outside.

A scorched and dazed Tracy realized that the Kid had saved his life.

Later, at City Hall, D.A. Fletcher coolly addressed the detective. "It's the word of you and a delinquent child against thirty-five witnesses."

"Are you telling me that if I pull in Big Boy Caprice, you won't prosecute?" Tracy asked.

"Fourteen witnesses insist Caprice spent the entire morning at a dance lesson," Fletcher insisted, walking away from Tracy.

That afternoon Tracy joined Tess, the Kid, and Chief Brandon at an unofficial ceremony in the detective's office. Chief Brandon gave the Kid a badge and an Honorary Detective Certificate, to be filled out when the Kid chose a name.

The Kid whispered to Tracy, "I've got something for you, too," and he returned Tracy's wallet and his badge.

"Put 'er there, Detective," Tracy said, shaking the Kid's hand.

Brandon asked Tess, "What about the orphanage?"

"We put it off till tomorrow," Tess answered.

That night, at a secret meeting in a cemetery, D.A. Fletcher complained to Big Boy. "It's Tracy. He's going to put two and two together. I killed his case against you, but that's the last thing I'm going to do, you hear me? I'm out."

Big Boy snarled, "I own you! You are mine! You are going to be the mayor of my city!" Big Boy jabbed his finger in Fletcher's chest. "You do what I tell you to do. When you're dead, that's when you're out…Mr. Mayor!"

Meanwhile, a faceless criminal was presenting a plan to piano player 88 Keys. "Tell Big Boy I'll get rid of Tracy for him," the Blank said, "in exchange for ten percent of his business."

Back at the Club Ritz, Big Boy complained, "Everywhere I turn it's Tracy, Tracy, Tracy, like he's reading my mind." What he didn't know was that above him in the attic, a man named Bug Bailey was listening to every word with a microphone that had been slipped through a hole in the ceiling. Thanks to Bug's reports from the club, Detective Tracy was able to ruin all of Big Boy's plans.

Between gang-busting arrests, Tracy was sharing some chili with Tess at Mike's Diner.

"You've got Big Boy on the run now. That's what you really care about," Tess said sadly. "I used to be afraid you would never settle down. Now I know it."

Before Tracy could answer, his wrist-radio crackled with the small, frightened voice of Bug Bailey.

"I understand. Go ahead, Tracy," Tess told him wearily, and Tracy bolted for the door.

Big Boy discovered the "leak" in his operation when Bug Bailey accidentally spilled coffee down the hole in the ceiling. Big Boy tricked Bug by faking a phone call in which he told his gangsters to hurry down to the Southside Warehouse. Then he had Bug dragged out of the attic.

Pruneface and Influence, two of Big Boy's thugs, were pouring cement over Bug Bailey when Tracy arrived at the warehouse. Tracy arranged his coat and hat behind some boxes to get the gangsters' attention while he rescued Bug.

Pruneface spotted the real detective and aimed his gun, but the Blank appeared out of nowhere and fired at Pruneface, saving Tracy.

Angered by the bungled trap, Big Boy was even more determined to get Dick Tracy. He decided to accept the offer presented by 88 Keys. The Blank would get rid of Tracy, and then Big Boy could get rid of the Blank.

Soon after, the Blank's fiendish scheme began to unfold. 88 Keys brought stolen samples of Tess Trueheart's and Dick Tracy's handwriting to someone who could copy them.

Meanwhile, in her childhood home, Tess was listening to her mother's sensible view of Dick Tracy.

"He could be President of the United States and call it a desk job," Mrs. Trueheart declared. "One day he's going to run out of luck. Real heroes always run out of luck."

Tess's heart was filled with love for Dick Tracy, a real hero. She decided to return to the City, where she stopped by the greenhouse to make a bouquet of flowers for him. There she was kidnapped by the Blank.

Tracy received a bouquet, but not from Tess. A forged note asked him to meet Tess at the greenhouse.

When Tracy got to the greenhouse, he was knocked unconscious by gas coming from jets beneath the flowers. The Blank had taken him prisoner.

Tracy woke up hours later in the Midway Hotel with a gun in his hand. The only other person in the room was a dead man, D.A. Fletcher, who was clutching a blackmail note written in Tracy's handwriting.

Since he was holding a weapon at the scene of the crime, Tracy was arrested for murder. The Blank and 88 Keys had successfully framed the detective.

At the Club Ritz, Big Boy rejoiced. "We're back in business, boys! I may run for mayor myself." With Tracy behind bars, Big Boy and his henchmen went on a crime spree.

Chief Brandon brought the Kid to visit Tracy in jail. Tracy was very happy to see them, but he was still upset that Tess had been kidnapped.

"I could find her in eight hours if I got back on the street!" Tracy said, pacing furiously.

"They should be coming to transfer you to County Jail in a little while," Chief Brandon said, leaving the Kid alone with Tracy.

The Kid proudly showed Tracy his permanent detective certificate, which contained the name he had chosen: Dick Tracy Jr.

Later, in the jailhouse parking lot, Tracy was delighted to discover his police escorts to be none other than Pat Patton and Sam Catchem. With the help of his loyal friends, Tracy had eight hours to rescue Tess.

Mumbles was very surprised when Tracy burst into his room that night.

Pat showed Mumbles the tape recorder concealed in the interrogation room's ceramic polar bear. As Tracy played back Mumbles's earlier betrayal of Big Boy, he fiddled with the machine so that Mumbles's words were clear.

"Who set me up?" Tracy demanded. "Talk, or I'll play your little song to Big Boy."

Suddenly Mumbles could speak as clearly as anyone. "Wait! 88 Keys, the piano man—he set you up. Big Boy paid him."

Armed with Mumbles's information, Tracy and his men sped to Big Boy's headquarters, the Club Ritz. Sam watched the building while Tracy and Pat climbed to the roof.

"Why are we going to the roof?" Pat asked.

"Always try to be on top of things," Tracy said, laughing. "That's where Big Boy is, and whoever framed me is framing him."

As they peered down through a skylight Pat and Tracy saw Tess Trueheart tied to a chair. Just then Big Boy and Flattop burst into the room and discovered her. But Flattop saw the detective and his partner and started shooting at them.

"Where did this dame come from?" Big Boy cried. "We've been framed! The cops are going to get us for kidnapping!"

The gangsters quickly untied Tess, taking her as a hostage.

At the same moment, the Blank called Chief Brandon at the police station to alert him to the kidnapping.

Tracy crashed through the skylight just as Flattop locked a metal door behind himself, Big Boy, and Tess. Tracy made rapid calculations, then moved a dresser and turned a trash can upside down. "Jump!" he yelled to the puzzled Pat.

Pat jumped onto one end of the dresser, and Tracy catapulted out of a second skylight. Far below, Chief Brandon's men were surrounding the Club Ritz.

Big Boy's gang panicked when they saw that the club was surrounded by cops. Big Boy shouted, "Lock the doors. Burn the records. Break out the guns! This is it!"

As the gangsters' cars charged the police line, tommy guns blasting, Big Boy led Tess through a secret door in the club's cellar. After jamming the door shut, Big Boy grabbed Tess and fled through a tunnel.

Tracy went after them, but he couldn't force the door. He guessed that they were heading for the river, and he rushed there in time to see Big Boy dragging Tess across the City Bridge.

Big Boy could see Tracy following him. When the drawbridge started to open to let a ship pass through, Big Boy pulled Tess into the gear house.

The gangster tied Tess to a giant gear wheel that was turning very slowly. When Dick Tracy entered the gear house, Big Boy aimed his gun at the detective. "Drop the gun, copper," he said, "or this next bullet's got your girlfriend's name on it."

"Don't do it, Dick!" cried Tess, even though each turn of the wheel brought her closer to her doom.

Tracy dropped his gun, and it went off, startling Big Boy. Tracy drove his heavy shoulder into Big Boy's soft belly and knocked the gangster to the floor beneath the gear wheel. As he turned to untie Tess he saw the Blank.

The faceless criminal pointed a gun at Tracy and at Big Boy, who was cowering on the floor. "I brought you down with kidnapping, Big Boy, the only crime you didn't commit," the Blank bragged.

"Whoever you are, maybe we can make a deal," Big Boy begged.

The Blank refused. "With you two out of the way, I'll own this town."

Tracy studied the Blank carefully. "I know who you are. I know what you've done. I know what you want, and it's not going to happen," Tracy declared.

The Blank aimed the gun at Tracy, but he couldn't pull the trigger. Suddenly the Kid popped up from behind some gears and tackled the Blank. Instantly, Big Boy retrieved his own gun and shot the Blank. Then Tracy charged after Big Boy and knocked him out with a powerful punch.

After Tracy hurriedly untied Tess, he asked her to call an ambulance. Then he went over to check on the Blank. "It was a great plan, Blank," Tracy said. "You almost pulled it off."

"Yeah. My only mistake was you," the Blank said with a sigh.

Later, at Mike's Diner, while Tracy, Tess, and the Kid were eating bowls of chili, the Kid finished explaining the case to Tess.

"88 Keys was a friend of the Blank's. That's how we got him to confess that the Blank killed D.A. Fletcher," the Kid concluded.

"You sound like a natural-born detective," Tess observed.

The Kid smiled. "I'm gonna be the greatest detective who ever lived!"

"You may be too smart to need this, but I'd like to give it to you anyway," Tracy said, giving the Kid a small wrist-radio.

While the kid played with his wrist-radio Tracy tried once again to propose marriage to Tess. But before he could get the words out, both wrist-radios crackled. "Calling Dick Tracy! Robbery in progress at Metropolitan Bank..."

"What are you waiting for, a desk?" Tess asked.

"Tess, you're one in a million," Dick Tracy said, smiling, as he tossed her a jewellery box.

Tess was admiring her engagement ring as Tracy and the Kid ran for the door.